LIFE SENTENCES

Richard Nelson

BROADWAY PLAY PUBLISHING INC
New York
www.broadwayplaypublishing.com
info@broadwayplaypublishing.com

LIFE SENTENCES
© Copyright 1993 Richard Nelson

Cover art by Zoe Nelson
First printing: December 2008
I S B N: 978-0-88145-408-6
Book design: Marie Donovan
Word processing: Microsoft Word
Typographic controls: Ventura Publisher
Typeface: Palatino

The End Of A Sentence (Part One of LIFE SENTENCES)
was first broadcast on American Playhouse Television
(Lindsay Law, executive producer) in Spring, 1991.
The role of BURKE was played by Edward Herrmann.
The director was David Jones; production designer,
David Jenkins; costume designer, Jane Greenwood;
lighting designer, Alan Adelman; and the producers
were Nondas Vaoll and Ellin Baumel.

LIFE SENTENCES was first produced by Second Stage
(Carole Rothman, Artistic Director; Suzanne Schwartz
Davidson, Producing Director) on 9 November 1993.
The cast and creative contributor were as follows:

BURKE . . . . Edward Herrmann
MIA . . . . Michelle Joyner

Director . . . . John Caird
Set designer . . . . Thomas Lynch
Costume designer . . . . Ann Roth
Lighting designer . . . . Richard Nelson

CHARACTERS & SETTING

BURKE, *forties, a college professor*
MIA, *twenties, his girlfriend*

Note: the locations should be minimally represented.

for Ed Herrmann

PART ONE
The End of a Sentence

Scene One

(A corner table of a bar in Penn. Station, New York City)

BURKE: Politics is coming back. *(He sips his drink.)* You can just feel it. It's in the air. I think it's because people are beginning to care again. It is caring itself that is coming back. *(Beat)* Politics and caring. *(Smiles)* It will be great. It'll be... *(He is lost in thought for a moment; suddenly he smiles to himself and laughs:)* They can push us liberals around only so long. And then! *(Laughs)* Then... *(Short pause)* If you wait long enough for something. If you only have the patience—. It will be great. *(Starts to sip his drink, but stops:)* I say this to Mia—. Mia's my—. We're a couple. We're not embarrassed to see ourselves as a couple. *(Beat)* I'm not. So I say this to Mia. That politics I think is coming back. And she says, "Don't tell me about it." *(He laughs a little too hard:)* Women! *(Laughs, then stops and tries to correct himself:)* Not all women. I didn't mean—. In fact in a lot of things women are just as— Most things. In really probably just about everything. In fact, I think women are probably better than men in every—. Just better than men. *(Beat)* This is one thing we've learned in the last twenty years. *(Beat)* I've learned it. *(Short pause)* I wasn't making fun of Mia. Not that she'd mind. She's got a great—. I was joking. She was joking. *(Forces a laugh)* She's very funny. When I first met her—.

Well, it took about two years of living together before
I was sure she wasn't all the time putting me down. She
has that sort of sense of humor. *(Laughs)* For example,
she tells everyone the only reason she moved in with
me was because I had a house and the school system
up in Dutchess County isn't so bad. *(Laughs)* She has a
daughter—that's what the bit about the school system
was referring—. Anyway, you get the sort of sense of
humor. *(Shakes his head.)* She's funny. And it's all done
with an absolutely straight face. *(Laughs)* She's subtle.
(Laughs. Pause. He sips his drink.) We met in a restaurant.
(Gestures: "like this one here.") A bar/restaurant. The bar
part of a restaurant. In the Village. I was completely
taken with her. One look and it was... I said to myself—
Burke, you could fall for this one. Really. And I have
never said this to myself before or since. Amazing.
(Beat) And she was taken with me too. I learned this
later. *(Beat)* I learned this about four or five years later.
Suddenly it just all of a sudden came out of her.
"Burke," she said, "remember that first time we met?
You know I was really taken with you." I was stunned
when she said this. I thought she was joking! *(Tries to
laugh.)* Anyway, even though she tries to hide it, I think
(whispers) that Mia is almost as far to the Left as me.
You cut through that tough—. What's inside—. The
caring, the feeling... She's quite instinctive about all this.
Like that, she cuts through the shit. On social issues,
I mean. Domestic—. As for foreign policy—. She
doesn't read newspapers, so—.

(Beat) Newspapers, it's sort of a thing of her's. A
conviction, you could call it. That's what she calls it.
Not to read newspapers. At first I thought she was
joking—. But— *(Beat)* She means it. *(Pause. Smiling:)*
What's funny is—. At first glance, you wouldn't think
Mia—. I mean, when I first introduced her to Reed—.
Reed's a friend. A very good friend. We go way back
together. He's one of those friends that you know you

will never ever lose. No matter what you do—.
No matter what he does—. And believe me, he can
be pretty damn obnoxious sometimes. *(Smiles)* Pretty
damn arrogant. He doesn't know half of what he thinks
he does. Every now and then I find myself putting
him in his place. *(Laughs)* I try not to, but—. *(Shrugs)*
His students love him. So he has that going at least. His
classes are packed. They love his theatrics, I suppose.
Students often do love that sort of thing. I like small
classes. *(Beat)* So most of mine are small. *(Beat)* Intimate.
That's where the real teaching can take place. I have
one class—Chaucer—with only five students. I had
limited it to fifteen, but five is even better. *(Short pause)*
Anyway...Reed and I are old friends, for better or
worse. And so we're often talking about—. I don't
know. The world. What's going on. Ideas. Trends.
And sometimes—. *(Laughs)* Sometimes we go on a bit
too long, I guess, and Mia immediately, instinctively
feels this and says: "Bullshit. What you are saying is
bullshit." *(Laughs)* It's hilarious! We love it. All of us
just love it! *(Pause. He stares off, then sips.)* I know what I
was saying. I was saying that when Reed first met Mia,
he thought... *(Sips again)* That it was only her beauty
that I was attracted to. The goddamn conclusions
people jump to! I was offended! I tell Reed that he
doesn't know anything because he hasn't seen her mind
yet. And I tell him—. This gets him. I tell him that there
are even times when I think Mia is even more to the
Left than me! Than us!!

(Beat) I say this and all hell breaks loose. *(Laughs:)* Reed.
Oh, Reed. But it's true. About Mia being more to the—.
I didn't just say it for effect. It is also true. About
domestic issues—. I didn't mean—. If she doesn't read
a newspaper—. But domestic issues, these she feels.
About these she has strong opinions and these opinions
are very, very to the Left. I can assure you. Trust me
on this one. *(Smiles)* On first meeting the two of us, you

wouldn't think we were alike at all! That's what people
tell me. But once you get to know us. Spend some time
together with the two of us... We both have beliefs.
Strong political beliefs. *(He looks at his watch and then
sips.)* One night while watching television—. Which we
do not do often. I don't. I like to read. Correct papers.
There are only so many hours in the day—. This
one night, amazingly we happened to be watching
television. Mia and me. Mia and me and her
seven-year-old daughter. And her daughter says
she wants to watch some cop show. I don't care. They
think I care, but I don't. One thing is just as stupid as—.
(Shrugs) You know, I have left my brain outside the
door-. Mia says, "If you don't want to watch!" When
have I said—? "Will you stop being, so goddamn
superior!" She says this. I want to say, "But I don't feel
superior, Mia. At least not to you. I consider ourselves
equals." I am formulating this in my head, looking
for the best way to express it, when Mia turns to her
daughter and says—. About the cop show, now. She
says— "They're shooting more blacks now." *(Beat)*
I say— "What??" And she turns back to me and says,
"They are shooting more blacks now than they used to.
On television." *(Beat)* At first I still don't get it. She
continues, "The criminals on these cop shows are
becoming more and more black again." *(Beat)* I am
stunned. I am really stunned, but she must take this
stunned expression for one of lack of interest or belief
because she says, "Oh, forget it." But I say, "Oh, no no
no." You see I am interested. This is the exact sort of
thing that does interest me! "Say more," I tell her. *(Beat)*
So she looks back and adds, "Also hispanics. They're
shooting more hispanics too." *(He shakes his head:)*
More blacks and more hispanics are being murdered
on television cop shows. And who noticed this? The
A C L U? No. Common Cause? No. *(Beat)* Here is an
observation worthy of a piece on the Times op-ed page

and who is the first to have made it? The N A A C P?
No. The last twelve years could be defined by this
one observation. Politically defined! And whose
observation is it?! *(Mouths: "Mia's")* And people have
looked at her like she wasn't smart!! *(Shakes his head)*
People can be so small. So very, very small and hurtful.
(Pause) Not everyone, of course. My first wife, Helen,
has always said—. From the very start she said that Mia
was just the right person for someone like me. She saw
us right away as a couple. I give her credit for that.
Of course, I first thought Helen was just being—.
She has a very mean sense of humor, I can attest to this.
And if you want to make fun of me, okay. Make fun of
me. This will not be hard to do. So at first I thought—.
Mia is after all a whole lot younger than Helen. Helen
and I were both in school—. All that stuff. All that
that means. But then I learned for a fact that she wasn't
making fun of me. No. It seems from the start she saw
the rightness of our relationship. How Mia and I have
things that Helen and I never could have had. Never
did have. And so it turned out, Helen meeting her
now-husband and moving with him to Sacramento—.
Moving our daughter there—. And then me meeting
Mia in the restaurant—. In retrospect, things work out.
They make sense. Things that at the time make no sense
whatsoever.... *(Beat)* Things that seem endless. And
ugly. *(Beat)* You live long enough and it all comes full
circle. It all seems to make perfect sense in time. When
that part is over. *(Short pause)* My daughter I now can
see all summer. We go fishing. Swimming. We drive
down here to the city and go to the Metropolitan.
I want her to experience culture, real culture, which
is a bit more than just the Indian weavings and totem
poles I gather they call culture in Sacramento. *(Beat)*
And we have family meals around a kitchen table that
I bought at an auction. *(Beat)* Mia loves my daughter.
They get along like sisters. Best friends, even.

Sometimes I look at her and I hold her hand and
I think—here is a child. Mia, I am talking about Mia.
She could be her sister. *(Laughs)* And then there's her
daughter. So there's also the mother-aura about her.
So there's both things. We're happy in the summer.
(Pause. Finally looks at his watch) Finally, in the end,
it is a very comforting thought. That politics is on its
way back. For years it's been—. For someone like me.
You start to wonder if you're mad. Out of step with
the goose-steppers, so to speak. *(Laughs)* But that old
pendulum swings, it had to. What goes around, comes
around. You see it in my students. *(Beat)* A few of my
students. Three or four. They have a curiosity again. For
a teacher you can ask no more. *(Pause. Looks at his watch
again)* Ten more minutes. I told him I'd meet him at the
information booth in ten minutes. At three. The train's
at three-fifteen. They open the gate fifteen minutes
early. It'll be empty. In the middle of the day in the
middle of the week it'll be very very empty. You'll be
able to get a sandwich and Coke—. Whatever you want
whenever you want. There'll be no line. I like empty
trains. *(Beat)* Like you're going someplace where no
one else is going. A few minutes yet. *(Short pause)*
I think this sort of thing is really important for the
kids—for the students. You really need to see things
from different points of view. This is what education
means, what it should mean. And that is what a
guest-speaker is all about. If he's the right one, that is.
If the person who has chosen the speaker—in this case,
me—if he or she has done his homework and so has
gone out of his or her way to insure that the speaker
is the right sort of speaker for the students and for this
time. *(Beat)* And if it were up to me, this kind of thing
would happen just about every day. We should be
teaching on the front lines. The front lines of art. The
front lines of...whatever. The more exposure to the real
world, the better. That's what I'm about. *(Beat)* You

know there's nothing—absolutely nothing in this for
me. In a money sense. I'm not paid a penny more. It's
even cost me a little. For lunch. For drinks. For waiting
around. Coming all the way into New York to meet
the guy, this was paid for. But the other things—.
But I used my time well. I went to the Metropolitan
and bought my daughter one of her birthday presents.
I'd get it out, but it's wrapped. It's a horse. A sculpture
of a Chinese horse. *(Beat)* It's wrapped. *(Short pause)*
Olek is going to be great. Sometimes you can just tell.
That French guy we had about two months ago. I
thought he was still supposed to be a Communist!
This is what I was told. This is how he was advertised.
(Shakes his head) Unbelievable the way people pass
themselves off. Or is it delude themselves. *(Beat)*
We had a Native American. He was good. Excellent.
Had a real anger in him. That's what the kids need to be
exposed to. Anger. Passion. *(Smiles:)* You won't believe
this, but Reed kept saying, "Keep him away from the
liquor!" Do you believe that? And Reed a liberal too.
(Smiles and shakes his head) I think it's Reed we should
have kept away from the liquor. But he means well.
Reed. And he always has. Not everyone knows this
about him. Anyway, the Indian was good. But the Frog
was bad. He'd like discovered investment banking the
week before and that is all this advertised Communist
wanted to talk about, and he was not talking about
it critically, let me tell you. *(Beat)* There was a former
South African white dissident. I do not know when
I have been so moved. The struggle, it was—.
Enormous is the only word for it really. He carried a —.
I would call it a profound moral weight with him.
Wow. *(Beat)* Lovely wife he had. Lovely accent. *(Beat)*
And then there was the Russian. Actually we could
have gotten any number of Russians. Busload and
busloads of Russians all for the asking and all for
next to nothing! *(Beat)* This one. The one we got—

I didn't choose him, I didn't have anything to do
with this one, he was a government department guest
speaker I think, or maybe it was history, I don't know.
I'm just glad he wasn't one of ours. This the English
department does not need. So this one, I think by the
time he'd left he'd scored like the third highest score
ever recorded on the Return of the Jedi video in
the games room, and this was only achieved by
considerable practice, let me tell you. I think his
sponsors—be they government or history—had to
something like crow-bar his fingers off that machine
to get him to where he had to speak. I mean, this is not
the kind of thing that helps, the kids should not see this;
this is not Russia. A guy playing video games is not
Russia! Even today! But—.

(Beat) Oh, well. You can't always—. *(Shrugs)* But
Olek will do just fine. He'll be terrific. After all Olek
Banouski, besides being a political dissident and
one-time Solidarity figure—when Solidarity was
banned, mind you—this is no johnny-come-lately—
we are talking about a real one-time political dissident—
but besides that, besides the politics, he is also a very
serious and highly-thought of novelist. In Poland.
(Beat) One of his books is being translated, he said.
Into English. *(Beat)* He's going to be great. He was
my first choice. Some of them in the department—.
Why is there so little imagination in your typical college
English department?? Why?!! *(Beat)* Three of my
colleagues—. I won't say who they wanted. And they
were about to succeed in getting him too, when I stood
up and said, "But we can get Olek Banouski! I can get
Banouski!" *(Beat)* "For about a third of what this guy's
going to cost!" *(Beat)* Eventually they agreed. First I
got them all to agree that Olek was a wonderful writer.
Even a great writer. They hadn't read a word he'd
written of course, but it's hard for a group of English
professors to admit something like that, so they

agreed—he was a terrific writer. Then the rest was easy. *(Beat)* So it was my choice. And he is going to be great. I have met him. Once. At a party. He is charming. His English is pretty damn good. Maybe he'll read a little from a translation. Whatever. He's coming; the signs are up announcing the lecture. Eleven tomorrow in the chemistry auditorium. Which is very comfortable. Very hospitable. It was available at eleven. I once gave a lecture there on the environment and the works of Joseph Conrad which came out pretty well if I do say so myself. *(Short pause. He drinks. Looks at his watch.)* He's probably waiting. I better go. *(Short pause)* I have the ticket. And I'll buy him whatever he wants on the train up. He's staying at my house. Our house. Mia's and my house. Mia's and her daughter's and my house. And he's going to sleep in Mia's daughter's room. Stuffed animals and all. *(Laughs)* He has two children, I believe, still in Poland, so this might be fun. *(Beat)* She's staying over with her friend, Patty. The dean's daughter. Lovely girl—the dean's daughter. *(Beat)* Mia is making us all dinner. Reed is coming over with his new girlfriend, who I think looks about eighteen, but in reality is two or three years older than Mia and this— I suspect-does not go down too well with her. *(Laughs)* Women. *(Shakes his head)* We'll have red wine. And vodka. I bought two bottles of Polish vodka. And we will talk. Tonight, we'll sit around the living room and talk. Is there any wonder why I'm feeling politics is coming back? *(Laughs to himself.)* Is there any wonder why I'm feeling so good? *(Sips his drink.)* We'll talk— Poland. Walesa. And Leftist politics. Yeltsin! Whatever. Everything and anything. We shall talk. About whatever comes up—. *(He finishes his drink:)* We'll talk.

(End of Scene One)

Scene Two

(The kitchen in BURKE's *house. As he speaks, he prepares a dessert.)*

BURKE: Both my first wife and Mia—my almost wife—love my zabaglione. Whenever there are guests—then it's out with everyone—out of the kitchen—and in with me. *(Smiles)* It's not hard to make, actually. A friend of mine in England showed me how. He was a classicist. Had a lovely wife. Still does!

*(*BURKE *laughs. From the other room—laughter)*

BURKE: That got a response. Something did. Anyway, when it comes to zabaglione, I'm treated like a genius! *(Prepares)* Everyone's having a terrific time. Olek is—. I think he's finally relaxed with us. After three or four vodkas I suppose he had no choice. *(Beat)* It's good to see him relaxing with—. With Americans, I guess I want to say. Seeing a different side to—. From what the rest of the world sees. Though it's not like we're the first—. Funny, I hadn't realized he'd actually taught. He was saying that that's how he in fact got to the U S. By teaching. Imagine: one day—he was in Paris—he'd gotten out just after marshal law was declared, it was that long ago, and he was in Paris and a letter arrives from of all places an American college—Bennington College. How they got his—? *(Shrugs)* So—would he teach a semester? This is what he is asked. How things happen in this world, you never ever know, do you? Sometimes it all seems just out of your hands. You can drive yourself crazy thinking—. If I hadn't gone into that restaurant—. I wouldn't have met Mia—. And so on and so on. Anyway, Olek went. It was in the winter. And he finds out, as he put it: *(In accent)* "Only girls go to this school." *(Laughs. Stops and corrects himself:)*

Women. I corrected him. We don't call them girls, I tell
him. Not anymore. *(Accent:)* "It was very bad winter,"
he says, "Much snow and these young girls—." He
didn't seem to get what I was saying. "These girls, they
had nowhere to go and nothing—to do." Then with
that very pixyish smile—he's a charming man—Mia is
fascinated with him—by his strangeness, I think—and
that's what having guest speakers, from the outside,
does for students—for us, the faculty, for those who
live on campus, near campus. I try to make this point.
I seem to make it over and over and over... *(Short pause)*
I was talking about Olek. He has this smile on his face
and he looks at me and says: "Bennington, best time of
my life." *(Beat)* I knew it was a good school.... I don't
know the school system in Poland. *(Beat)* But I thought
he still was exaggerating, so I asked him if it was even
a better time than when he first met Lech Walesa.
He says that is like comparing apples and cherries.
(Laughs to himself) Apples and cherries. *(Short pause)*
After Bennington, he taught at a few more schools
for women. I forget which—. They weren't nearly as
prestigious. He listed three or four. "Only for girls!"
He kept saying. Odd to hear someone still call them
"girls." I guess maybe in Europe. *(Pause)* All in all,
I think he's having a lovely time with us. Reed's
behaving himself. And his girlfriend hasn't said a
word about Olek's smoking. I guess maybe because
he's European she doesn't dare. I haven't seen someone
chain-smoke in—. Anyway, you can still smell Mia's
bread. She baked bread. As soon as we walked in—.
I love that. I'll bet Olek must have loved that. Walking
into a strange house and smelling—. He must have
known then he was among decent people. People of
the land. *(Beat)* You can still smell it here in the kitchen.
(Smells. Takes a sip from his drink on the counter) You
don't think—. *(Beat)* No. He wouldn't. A teacher—
even a temporary one—has a responsibility to—. I

mean, if what he's saying—and this has just occurred
to me—perhaps I had not at first understood—if
he's saying that he only taught at schools for women
because... *(Beat)* He's got a wife and two children in
Warsaw. He is going to bring them here. Someday,
he said. As soon as he gets the cash together. Which
is why he teaches. At women's colleges. Look, I don't
want to judge—. It is actually none of my business.
Also, remember it's probably a lot different if you're
not tenured, if you're only—. Just for one semester, then
there's a whole different—. Students must know you'll
be leaving. They send out signals. It's probably easy
to fall into the trap. *(Beat)* And—he's European. And
I think Europeans—Eastern Europeans, let's stick just
with that. England after all is Europe too, and they're
not at all like this, but Eastern Europeans have a whole
different take on some things than we do. We haven't
had to live through wars like—. To live and suffer as,
say, Sartre has said: "for the moment." No doubt one
learns a different ethos. Different rules, both intellectual
and... *(Beat)* Look: as long as his wife doesn't find out.
(Laughs) That's if she cares. Maybe she—! Maybe that's
how—! *(Laughs)* The world is a big big place, isn't it?
And this is why we have guest speakers. *(Pause as
he prepares) (To himself:)* "Like comparing apples and
cherries." *(Looks up:)* And I corrected him. But now
I think "cherries" is what he really meant. *(Laughs to
himself)* Mia finds him interesting. She isn't put off.
And that's a good thing. *(Pause)*

Enough of that. It was just this afternoon, wasn't it,
that I was saying that I thought politics was coming
back. Well, sitting over dinner, while the others were
talking—. Some of the things that got brought up.
We were really swinging for a while. Not just Poland.
There was Bosnia. China. Africa. There was the
difference between a senator and a representative.
While I was listening—. When it was my turn to listen. I

had talked enough. I got to thinking—looking at their faces now—I thought it's not exactly that politics is coming back; it's that politics has never really left us and that is now what we are realizing. It's a subtle difference, but an important one. *(Beat)* I'm not saying this is true for everyone, but for us. And I have to admit it makes me feel a lot better. If it's only that politics is coming back then we're still waiting for it, but if it's already with us, but just has been sort of hibernating or not being as—obvious, maybe is the word—then I for one feel a whole lot more comfortable with myself. And that's half the point, isn't it? Half of what we're talking about. *(Beat)* Politics has never left us—people like us—and now we are again coming to understand that. Look at Reed. Let's start with him. This man is still concerned about the world. We all see that now. Reed, after all, single- handedly formed the Amnesty International Club on campus. He himself sat for half of one day at a table just outside the cafeteria in a metal helmet like they used to use to torture prisoners in Iranian prisons. Nearly everyone signed the protest petition. That's Reed. He's easy. Now then there's his girlfriend, who even though she's from a much later generation and she looks even younger than that— especially tonight in those pants she's wearing. *(Smiles)* She's got the figure for them. *(Quickly adding:)* So does Mia. Both of them—great figures. *(Short pause. He listens.)* I thought I heard someone coming. I thought maybe Mia... *(Shakes his head)* Those pants do make her look more like one of Reed's—or my—students than his—. His whatever; girlfriend, I guess I can call her. Actually, she was a student of mine about seven years ago. Reed never had her then. *(Corrects himself)* She was never in one of Reed's classes. I had her in composition. *(Corrects himself)* I taught her composition. I don't know why she never took—. Maybe she didn't like Reed then. Maybe she'd heard something bad about his courses.

(Laughs) I do think they're serious. At least I think he is.
Mia and I, what we have here, I think this has spurred
him on. To get serious. With someone. *(Beat)* I'd like to
think we did that. *(He stares.)* I like her a lot. I like the
way her mind works. She has a real sense of the absurd.
And she's good with Reed. Keeps him in his place.
Like Mia does with me. *(Beat)* Anyway, back to my
point—sitting next to her watching reports on the
T V about the oil spill in Scotland, with those birds
all covered in black being pulled out of the goo—.
Watching her, it broke my heart. She was nearly
hysterical. She really cared. *(Beat)* Reed had to take
her for a long walk. *(Short pause)* The politics—the
passions—they're in us all right. They are already in us.
And from time to time they can't help but come out.
(He prepares and thinks to himself.)

(End of Scene Two)

Scene Three

(The kitchen. BURKE *hurries in with a tray of empty drinks.)*

BURKE: We're already on the second bottle of vodka.
(Beat) We started on vodka. Then went to wine for
the meal. And now we're back to vodka. *(Laughs; short
pause as he pours more drinks)* He has us on the edge of
our seats, by the way. Story after story about what he's
gone through. *(Beat)* His escape from marshal law was
chilling beyond belief. It's like having a hero of some
revolution in your own living room. *(Beat)* I doubt if
I'll ever forget tonight. We won't let him stop talking.
(Finishes pouring and hurries out with the drinks)

(End of Scene Three)

Scene Four

(Outside. Night. BURKE *sits alone, a drink at his side.)*

BURKE: *(He watches the sky; sips his drink; then:)* It was only a kiss, for Christ sake. Now she's gone to bed. I'm pretty sure it was him, anyway. My guess is that she was sitting there, listening to him talk on and on and on about Solidarity and Polish literature and whatever, and he mistook her interest in—. Mistook her rapt attention for—. *(Beat)* So he kissed her, and that is what I happened across, when I happened to come back into the kitchen. *(Beat)* We are talking about happenstance here. Luck. *(Beat)* Mia has explained this. *(Beat)* Just by her look to me when she went off to bed, this explained it. *(Beat)* Just by the hug she gave me. By the hug she gave me back when I hugged her. This explained... *(Beat)* She has trouble sleeping. I think women often do. So every night before going to bed she makes herself some hot water. Just hot water. Every night before going off to bed she goes into the kitchen to make herself hot water. Every night she's in the kitchen doing this. I tell her she should have an electric kettle in the bedroom. *(Beat)* So she wouldn't have to go to the kitchen late at night—in her nightgown. Where it is cold. *(Pause.)* It is not so cold tonight. A very clear night. Cool. Crisp. But not cold. He's certainly a charming fellow. Olek. *(Beat)* Olek Banouski. Quite the name. *(Laughs to himself)* Irresistible, I would suppose. One of those guys who has all the moves down. But when you scratch the surface—. Anyway, Reed I think is being a bit hard on him in there. I've known Reed for—; and once he gets started. He's a fighter. He loves a good—. But still, to come right out and say to Mister Olek Banouski—okay, so why don't you go back to Poland?! *(Laughs)* That's not really fair, is it? Not to

say he didn't ask for—. But the man is a guest in my
home. *(Beat)* Olek seems to take it all in good stride.
Which is fortunate. Seems he likes to argue as much
as—. I mean the level of discussion going on in this
house right now—. This is something one lives for.
Olek is right now in there saying for the tenth time
that by staying here in America he is doing the right
thing for his family and friends. While Reed keeps
saying—he would go back if he were Polish and he
could now go back—like Olek. Olek seems to find
Reed amusing. *(Beat)* So he doesn't seem to be offended.
Which is good. You don't invite people into your home
just to—. Reed should know this. But—.

(Beat) Would I go back to Poland if...? *(Shrugs)* How can
one answer that? How could Reed? There is so much
we cannot know. About ourselves. About what we are
feeling or how we would feel if—. Even then, emotions
can sometimes be quite confusing. Sometimes you don't
know what you think, or should think, or—. *(Short
pause)* Olek is a bit lost, I think. As a person, he is lost.
This happens to all of us at one time or another. I would
be lost too if I were in his shoes. Very understandable.
The whole thing. Everything. I blame no one. And this
is right. This is fair. *(Beat)* Reed should be easier on him.
I'll apologize for Reed after he's left. *(Reaches down and
picks up his glass, takes a sip. As he drinks:)* The level of
discussion—! Who the hell said you had to live in,
say, New York City or Greenwich Village to have
discussions at this level?! I'll tell you who—my first
wife thought this and then she met this guy who moved
her to Sacramento! *(Laughs)* Every time I think about it
I laugh! *(Pause)* Mia loves it here. And her daughter is
very happy. Very, very happy. Neither can complain.
(Looks at watch) One o'clock. He better get to bed soon.
He's lecturing tomorrow. He better get some sleep.
None of us are as young as we think we are. *(Looks at
the stars)* Wonder what time it is in Poland. Where his

family his—his wife and two children. Must be morning. Sometime in the morning. *(Beat)* Peasants in red kerchiefs, standing in line to buy food. Intellectuals having coffee. Crowded trolleys. Steam. Sounds of people, a large crowd of people walking to work. The sound of them walking. Factory whistle. Where do we get these pictures? Where do I get these images from? Where? I don't know. *(Beat)* I'm told teachers there are respected about like priests. *(Shakes his head)* I don't know who told me this. *(Looks off into the sky)* In, say—China now? You can imagine— clandestine meetings between fugitive student and fugitive teacher. Bicycles hidden in bushes. *(Looks at his watch again)* It's like in the afternoon there, I think. Or is it tomorrow night already? *(Beat)* In Russia... In South Africa... In. *(Short pause)* It's all very exciting. Very, very exciting. Important things are happening. One can sit in one's own backyard and feel it all happening out there. *(He sips.)*

(A burst of laughter from inside. BURKE *looks toward the house.)*

BURKE: I think I hear Mia with them. *(Beat)* I guess she couldn't sleep. *(Short pause. He takes off his glasses and rubs his eyes.)*

(End of Scene Four)

Scene Five

(BURKE's *study; the middle of the night.* BURKE *sits in an arm chair. A book is in his lap.*)

BURKE: Whenever I can't sleep, I read. *(Short pause)* When Susan was four—this was while everyone was still here, together, and before the move first to Greenwich Village and then to, of all places, Sacramento. *(Laughs)* When my daughter was four, I would buy her a book every week. I'd go with her and—. She'd choose. That was half the lesson I was trying to teach. How to choose. *(Beat)* One a week. On Saturday. Allowance day. To the book store. This way she learned how to make a judgment—. In time she learned this. You try your best with your children. What else can you do? *(Shrugs. Short pause)* Books and books and books. There they all are. What one knows. *(Smiles)* A lot of books. *(Nods)* A lot of good times. *(Silence)* Everyone's finally asleep. As I came down the steps past Mia's daughter's room I could hear Olek snoring. In fact, from the moment he took his last sip of vodka to closing the door to the room behind him—. This could not have been—. The time, maybe fifteen seconds. And then— snores. Right out of the room. He must still have his clothes on. I didn't check. *(Beat)* I didn't think I should check. *(Beat)* Mia said she'd check. I told her not to bother. *(Pause.)* Right as Reed and Barbara were leaving—. They called, by the way, they did get home. Barbara drove and I was not in favor of this. I told them they should have stayed. There's room. They could have stayed here in the study. You take risks and then one day—. *(He hears something upstairs.)* What's—?? Footsteps. Someone's up. *(Listens.)* Sounds like Olek. Like a man's—footsteps. Must be going to the bathroom. After all he's had to—.

I'm not surprised. *(Beat)* I hope he doesn't wake up Mia.
That was the bathroom door. Sh-sh. Mia's a light
sleeper. *(Short pause)* What was—? Reed and Barbara.
Now they are home. In Reed's home. She's trying to
move up here, I just found this out tonight. Reed is
hesitating. I would have thought it was the other way
around. The way he's talked to me about her—. He's
totally taken with—. But you never know. People
don't always tell you the truth. *(Beat)* They hide things.
(Pause) Olek. *(Listens, then continues:)* As Reed was
leaving, Olek finally started to—. This was incredible.
It'll sound a little cliché, but what he did was—open up.
Open his heart up to us. Whatever he was doing—
whatever you want to call this, which was not a pose or
anything, it was real, very real, well—it broke us all up.
Just like that from talking about Polish poetry to—.
Without even a beat, he starts talking about his little
daughter. Or not so little daughter now. In Poland.
It's been a few years now since... You begin to see a
whole other side to the man. The father and husband
side. What he has sacrificed. The wound he has. He had
us in tears. Barbara, she couldn't control herself. Reed
had to take her for a short walk. *(Beat)* Mia had gone
back to bed so she missed—. She'd been up and down
I think ten times, but here—. I don't know what her
problem is. But at this point she wasn't there. She was
in bed. *(Beat)* I'll tell her about it in the morning. She'll
be amazed. She'll be very moved to hear about his
daughter and his wife in Poland. He even translated
part of a letter she'd written him. His daughter had
written to Olek. *(Beat)* There is so much pain in the
world. And so little we can do about it. *(Pause)* So—
if we're looking for an explanation for his behavior.
With Mia. When she was about to push him away in
the kitchen as he tried to kiss her... He is a desperately
sad and lonely man. *(Beat)* I have Mia, but what does
someone like Olek Banouski have? *(Beat)* I have Mia

and her daughter. *(Short pause)* I mean, what would
I be like if I didn't have Mia? If suddenly—. If for
political reasons we were—. You start to think this
way—you force yourself to be fair to other people
and not too quick to judge them. Or what they do.
(Short pause) I think everyone had a good time tonight.
I mean how often—in America—does one have the
chance to let down one's hair and talk about—. To talk
to—! And then to have him open up. I was honored.
And I think Reed and Barbara felt the same way. A
good night. *(Beat)* Talk and talk and more talk. After a
day like today, who wants to go to sleep? Or who can?
(He hears something upstairs.)

(End of Scene Five)

Scene Six

*(BURKE's office at the college; afternoon of the next day.
BURKE at his desk with a book of poetry in front of him.*

BURKE: *(Reads from the book:)* "Over the carnage rose
prophetic a voice, Be not dishearten'd, affection shall
solve the problems of freedom yet, Those who love
each other shall become invincible, They shall yet make
Columbia victorious." *(He looks up.)* I had the student
who was just here read this. I'm quizzing her to see if
she knows who wrote it. I figure she'd pick Whitman
in a second because of the rhythm. But after she reads:
"They shall yet make Columbia victorious" for the
third time, she guesses it's by some guy who goes to
Columbia University. *(Laughs)* Sometimes they make
you feel so damn smart. *(Smiles and shakes his head;
closes the book.)* So—it was a fiasco, by the way. Olek
Banouski's lecture—if that is what one could call it.
In fact, one would have to be incredibly generous—
or perhaps just criminally ignorant—to call it anything
but a swear word. *(Beat)* The dean's already told me the

next time I propose someone to guest lecture, I will have to have three other professors to co-sponsor as well. *(Beat)* In other words, my recommendation is now under the cloud of suspicion thanks to the rather unbelievable and unforgettable performance this morning of our Polish friend. And I have to admit that all such suspicion is more than justified. *(Beat)* It is a good thing I have tenure, let me tell you. *(Short pause)* Actually, I should have known—in fact, I started to guess we might have a problem when this rather heavily hung over fellow met me in the hallway this morning, wearing, as I had guessed, the clothes he had slept in all night and worn all the day before. *(Beat)* Here was our conversation. "Good morning, Olek, how'd you sleep?" To this he replies, "Did we finish the vodka?" I ignore this and ask if he'd like to use the bathroom first. He seems not to even hear me and wanders off—I suppose now in retrospect—to look for the vodka. *(Beat)* After I have my shower I hurry downstairs to rustle up a big pot of strong black coffee, thinking this will do the trick. *(Beat)* After four or five cups, we seem to be moving in the direction of the door and I remind him, "Don't forget your notes!" "What notes?" he answers. "For your lecture this morning, Olek." "I have no notes," he says. Then— "I need no notes." He says this just as Mia enters now in her nightgown. I don't know why she felt she knew Olek well enough to wander around the house in her blue nightgown. That's the one that is quite short. But obviously it doesn't bother her. So she does. I suggest that she go and get dressed. She kisses me on the cheek. She kisses Olek also on the cheek. I say we should be going. Right now. *(Beat)*

"Say goodbye to Olek," I say to Mia. Finally, after some goodbyes and an exchange of phone numbers— I keep telling Olek he can call me at school, he has that number, but they exchange numbers. Then I get him

into the car. And get him to the campus. *(Beat)* And
I help him into the chemistry auditorium. And there
are about sixty or so students; Reed comes in just
before we start and sits way in the back with his feet
up over another seat. Thank you, Reed. Thank you.
(Beat) I introduce Olek. I give him a very, very warm
introduction. I call him a personal friend. Which at this
point I think he is, after having stayed at my house and
talking for most of the night. A personal friend. Both
my friend and Mia's friend. A family friend. *(Beat)*
The microphone works fine. There is no problem there.
(Beat) And so it begins. The fiasco begins and ends soon
thereafter. He says about twenty maybe thirty almost
incomprehensible words, one of which has something
to do with Bennington College. *(Beat)* After five, seven
minutes, he says that is it, folks. Thanks. No, he doesn't
even say thanks. Just smiles that insincere smile of
his and nods. Well, I jump up and say something like,
"Short but sweet!" Ha ha. *(Beat)* Ha ha. And ask for
questions. Nothing. I look at Reed. Nothing. Thank you,
Reed. Thanks. So I ask him if he wants to discuss
the difference between Polish culture and American
culture. *(Beat)* As he has found them. *(Beat)* He says,
no, he doesn't. *(Beat)* Then, sensing my panic, I
suppose, he offers to read from the book that is being
translated. Read from the translation. I breathe a sigh
of relief. So he did have something planned. Hallelujah!
Hallelujah! Hallelujah! I introduce the book in glowing
terms, I haven't read it. But it's a good introduction
and he starts to read. *(Beat)* I'm being kind. He starts
to something. Because you see Olek Banouski doesn't
really read English. I don't mean he doesn't read it well.
It is very, very difficult for him to read English out
loud. I now know this about him. And I am now not
the only person who knows this about him. *(Beat)*
Also—every fifth word or so—that is, after trying
to sound out every fifth word or so—he'd stop and

question the translation. This appeared to be the very
first time he had ever read it. So he would stop and
explain to his very uninterested audience how what
he had written meant something else. But usually he
misunderstood the English so pretty much all of what
he said—should one have been listening—made no
sense. In other words, this part of his presentation
was less than dynamic. *(Beat)* I let him go on for
about forty-two minutes like this, letting his audience
dwindle to a handful of the stunned, sick, or asleep.

(Phone rings.)

BURKE: Just a second. *(Picks up the phone; into the phone:)*
Hello? *(Short pause)* Okay, okay. Call me back when you
can stop laughing. *(Hangs up)* That was Reed. My good
friend. *(Beat)* The luck some people have. When his
Iranian guy, the speaker his Amnesty club sponsored,
was here he came not only with slides and tapes of
indigenous music, but also with that metal torture
helmet I told you Reed wore for a week outside the
cafeteria. I mean, he was prepared; and this was a guy
Reed had never even met! Got the name out of some
magazine, I think. *(Beat)* It's just not fair. Let me tell
you, it'll be a long time before I get involved in Eastern
Europe again. *(Short pause)* So—let me finish. First, no
one came up to Olek after his quote unquote talk. I have
never seen that happen before. No one. Even I didn't
want to go up to him, but I still had the responsibility
of getting him on the train. So I did. *(Beat)* So I drove
him to the station, where I can't find a parking spot—
which happens—so I just drop him off. He has about a
twenty-five minute wait. *(Beat)* I give him his check—
which now should come under the heading of "stolen
goods" —smile a lot, a whole lot, pat him on the back,
until he finally says: "Burke, it has been fun." *(Beat)*
Fun. *(Beat)* What I really want to say to him is—I don't
know what sort of colleges they have where you come

from, but here we're interested in a lot more than just
"fun"! *(Beat)* But I figure what's the point. *(Beat)* So he
wanders off in the direction of the station and that is
the last I see of Olek Banouski. That is the end of him.
(Laughs:) "It's been fun"!! Unbelievable. *(Beat)* Olek
Banouski. I won't soon forget that name. He had his
chance and he blew it. There we were, ready to listen.
And—. What a pity. What a waste. That's what
finally hurts. *(Short pause)* Funny how we keep being
disappointed in life. We hope someone, something
is going to be—. Going to help, and then—. *(Shrugs)*
Again and again and again and again. *(Short pause;*
he suddenly notices a photograph of MIA *in the frame on*
his desk. He picks up the photo.) An old picture. I'm going
to get a new one taken. One of the both of us—that's
what I want. The two of us together. *(He sets the photo*
down.) How did I—? *(He tries to remember:)* Oh, right.
I was saying something about how politics is coming
back. Well—it is. I just picked the wrong day—the
wrong person—with which to make my point. But
it's definitely coming back, I swear. And it'll be great.
(Short pause as he opens the poetry book again. He reads:)
"Over the carnage rose prophetic a voice. Be not
dishearten'd, affection shall solve the problems of
freedom yet, Those who love each other shall become
invincible, They shall yet make... Columbia victorious."
(Beat. Laughs:) "Columbia." They make you feel so
damn—. *(He mouths the word "smart") (Long pause)*
I love teaching. *(Beat)* I love talking. *(Beat)* To people
who listen. *(Beat)* Even to people who have to listen.
(Smiles, looks back down at the book)

END OF PART ONE

PART TWO
The Beginning of a Sentence

Scene One

(The garden. The afternoon of the lecture. MIA *is on her knees gardening; after a moment, she sighs, wipes her face, leans back, and looks up:)*

MIA: I love gardening. In my family, it's what one did when the world just got too complicated. *(Beat)* We did a lot of gardening. Everywhere I lived, we had a beautiful garden. Flowers, vegetables... It's real. No bullshit. You sow what you plant; see what you grow; eat what you harvest. What could be simpler? My mother used to say that in her life that she'd spent a lot more "quality" time with vegetables than with men. *(She pulls out a weed.)* I used to garden with my mother. When I was a girl. It was a special time between us. No one else to complicate anything. *(Beat)* Just us. *(Beat)* I still hear her voice when I'm falling asleep. Still see her face—the face of my mother when I was a small kid. She'd even tell me bedtime stories that had a gardening theme and that always ended with the young sapling growing toward the sun—reaching for the sun. Or some variation of this. It was her effort to instill in me some sense of direction. Ever since I was a kid I have tried hard to be a sapling reaching for the sun. *(Beat)* Whatever that means. *(Beat)* My mother used to say gardening makes the world clearer. Just to see a new bud, she'd say, makes sense out of so much else. *(Beat)*

When she dies, I'm going to make certain there are
potted plants with fresh buds among the cut flowers,
just as I have seen her do at a relative's funeral a few
years ago. *(Beat)* Burke doesn't garden. All of this I
have done by myself. *(Looks over her garden and smiles)*
Though he's bought me many beautiful books about
gardening. In fact, we have one whole shelf in the
kitchen devoted just to the beautiful gardening books
that he's bought me. I tell him—enough's enough, but
the books keep coming. A couple are so big, they don't
really fit; I tell him, Burke, they're called "coffee table
books" for a reason. But he tries to jam them into that
shelf. *(Beat)* We're different people. He brought home
one gardening book, it must have been three feet long.
I'd never seen such a book. "That must have cost a
fortune," I said. "Only forty dollars," he said, "look
here." And then he opened up the book and half of the
pages had been printed upside down, that's why he
said he got it for half off. *(Beat)* I said— "It sure looks
like you got a deal, Burke." And he smiled, and then
I watched him look through this great big book and
every few pages he had to turn it upside down. Finally
we just cleared off the kitchen table of everything—
salt shakers, everything—so he could just sort of spin
it around to read it and not hurt his arms, which he
already had carrying the thing home. *(Beat)*

What a book, I told him. *(Beat)* Different people. *(She
gardens for a moment.)* There came the point of course
when we stopped doing anything together. My mother
and me. This is common. Mothers and daughters. *(Beat)*
So I've read—in a book that Burke bought me. A small
book. I kept it on my bedside table for at least a year.
Once Burke, to be funny, I think, wrote with his finger
in the dust on the book jacket: "Read 'Me." *(She smiles.)*
I've planted peas, carrots, green beans, and fourteen
different kinds of flowers. My mother sent me the
flower seeds—with a note saying, now that she'd

met Burke and seen where Susan and I were living—
she'd visited us for the first time last Christmas—
she said that she knew that I'd be wanting to do a lot
of gardening. *(Beat)* Mothers. *(Pause, then looks up)*
It was while gardening, in fact, that my mother—.
She stopped what she was doing—. I was fifteen then.
She stops and takes a sip of her drink—a Manhattan,
it must have been—and she says "Dear, I've been
waiting years for a chance to explain." *(Beat)* I look at
her—remember: fifteen—and ask, "What do you mean,
Mom? Explain what?" "Oh dear," she says, "Where is
a soul to begin?" *(She sits back, opens a thermos and pours
herself a drink.)* "You know your Grandfather Herbert,
don't you?" she asks. "Of course I know him, Mom!
What are you talking about?" For fourteen of my
fifteen years we'd lived down the block from my
grandparents—my father's parents. They'd taken
a responsible interest in us, everyone said, ever since
my rotten son-of-a-bitch father, quote unquote, left
us for that purpled-lipped banshee, quote unquote,
fourteen years ago. "What are you talking about,
Mom?" *(Beat)* Another sip of Manhattan. It was a
hot day. "Well, your grandfather Herbert, your father's
father," she continued, "think of it this way, as I think
of it. Think of him not as your grandfather, which,
by the way, he isn't." "What?" I say. "Think of him,
well—as your father, since that is what he is." *(Short
pause)* Then she looked at the garden and said, "I think
I should have planted marigolds instead." *(Beat)*
"I don't understand," I say. "Herbert's your father,
dear—are you deaf?" *(Beat)* "Marigolds or maybe
nasturtiums. Look, Mia," she says to my face now
and knew she had to say something, "I'd hoped not
to complicate this for you, but if you are going to
insist—the man who I was married to is Herbert's son;
so if you wish to be pedantic about it, I suppose instead
of being your father, he's really your step-brother. And

then there's your grandmother—who, bless her, did
not leave Herbert when she found out, but instead
I think we both would agree she's cooked us some
very nice meals over these past fourteen years, well,
she I suppose in some way may be your grandmother,
I was legally married to her son after all, though she
is also your step-mother, being married as she's been
these past fifty-two years to your father. I think that's
right. Step-mother. Yes. You see, even I get confused."
And she laughed. *(Beat)*

"I don't want to confuse you, dear, but as you asked,"
I remember feeling quite dizzy from the heat as she
continued, "the man who you thought was your father
and who now you know to be your step-brother—
or is it half-brother—well, and you should know this—
he didn't leave you for a banshee—she came later—
we only used her as an excuse to—I don't know—
make you feel better. Like there was a reason for things.
No, he found out about—me and his dad, whom
I loved very much for a while. You were a true child
of love, Mia, and that is what is important, after all.
(Beat) Fifteen. *(She gets back down on her hands and knees
and gardens. Looking up)* My newfound father, by the
way, was then seventy-three, a distinguished professor
of romance literature—appropriate. My mother had
been a student of his as well as his daughter-in-law.
Not once, she told me proudly, throughout the entire
year of his class did he show any favoritism toward
her—even though she was his daughter-in-law and she
was sleeping with him. As she said— "distinguished".
The Provencal poets, I understand, was his specialty—
among other things. *(Beat)* When he knew that I knew
he asked me to start calling him "Dad" —but only
in private as, he said, his wife had already suffered
enough. I was encouraged by everyone to spend more
time now with "Dad," who everyone agreed had much
to teach me. I was even given a room of my own in

their handsome home, where I would spend my
weekends. It was large and beautifully wallpapered,
with a view of their garden and a lock on the inside of
the door that I bought with my own allowance money.
And Mother began dating again—mostly older college
professors—her type—whom she met in bars away
from the campus; and so on weekends at least, when
she had the house to herself, she provided a necessary
service among those walls of ivy—as a piece of mortar
for a stray leaf or two to grab onto. *(Pause, lost in
thought, then:)* How did I—? I was talking about...?
Gardening. I was thinking about gardening. *(Beat)*
My mother used to say it's no coincidence that the
Bible begins in a garden. When she'd say this, I used
to say, "I wonder if Adam and Eve had a thermos of
Manhattans." And she'd say, "If it was paradise—they
did." *(Beat)* Last night, when everyone was praising my
bread, I said—the peas, I froze them, they're from last
year's garden! Reed couldn't believe it. Barbara said
she usually doesn't like frozen peas, but these were
different. *(Beat)* Mister Banouski—Olek—said that
his wife too had a garden back in Poland. You have to,
he said, just to eat. *(Beat)* In such places, things must
be simpler—you do what you do because you have
to—you don't need any other reason. *(Beat)*

The lecture should be over by now. I hope it went well,
Burke was so looking forward to showing Olek off.
(Beat) He's a handsome man—worth showing off,
I would think. And all the things he's done, it puts us
to shame. Last night—talking to him in the kitchen—
watching him talk. I sat up on the kitchen counter so
I could be more his height—. He helped me up. Boosted
me *(Beat)* I think there's a kind of love that only lasts
a few hours—like a flower that only blooms for one
morning, and then closes up. Then one goes back to
a different kind of love—a love that is lasting, that
could even be forever. *(Beat)* He reminds me—Olek—

a little of Susan's father. He had been my high school
French teacher. The same lonely look and the accent.
He wasn't French, but he'd spent most every summer
in Quebec, so—. That's how he said he got the accent.
He was from Missouri. He smoked too—like Olek.
Funny, last night—it seemed right. No one said
anything about the smoking, not even Barbara. I've
opened the windows now, but last night. By tonight his
smell—the smell will be gone. Susan won't even notice
it; if she does she can stay in her room if she doesn't like
it. The world does not revolve around children. *(Beat)*
The whole evening—it reminded me of a foreign film,
the smoking, the accent—. I kept thinking, I'm in a
foreign film. *(Realizes:)* That's why I was thinking of
my daughter's father—my French teacher—we used
to go, he'd take me to see foreign films. Never before
had I—. But I went with him. I learned to love different
languages and different places. It's how I learned that
nudity was artistic. These films and my French teacher
taught me this. We used to go out after them and over
a Coke and a sandwich or a burger, we'd discuss them.
It was like getting a free education. That's what he said.
(Beat) I remember in one there was a girl, woman really,
and she charges into her apartment, knocks down a
wall, and there is her roommate—naked, on a toilet
with this guy on her lap and they are doing it; she's
holding him so it stays in and they are humping on
the toilet seat. *(Beat)* I remember wondering: how could
they fake that? Were they wearing a kind of body
stocking? My French teacher said he thought it was
for real. That what we thought was happening—
was happening. *(Beat)* It was from Yugoslavia, I think.
The movie. *(Beat)* Where there now is only war, right?
(Shakes her head) So when my French teacher asked me
if I thought what these— "people," he called them,
because if they were really doing it they weren't
"actors," he said, but "people" like—us; whether,

what these people were doing was—well, bad. I said
I didn't think it was either bad or good, but rather—
it was true. *(Beat)* He said that if I wrote an essay in
French and said that, he'd give me an A-plus easy.
(Smiles) I never wrote the essay. *(Beat)* I got pregnant.
Left school. Susan was born. My almost-father—the
one who had left us and was my real father's son and
therefore only my step-brother—he helped with the
expenses. And he didn't have to do anything, what
was I to him? He'd been studying to be a doctor when
I was born, but when he left my mother he decided he
wanted to be a psychiatrist instead so now he had lots
of money and he helped. *(Beat)* Susan and I had the best
of everything. *(Smiles)* Mother said when she visited
that she didn't get a private room when I was born!
(Laughs to herself) (Beat) My French teacher had to leave
his job. He decided to go pick grapes in California,
it's what he said he always wanted to do. *(Beat)*

So, he said, I shouldn't feel sorry for him. *(Pause, lost in
thought, then:)* How did I— *(Remembering:)* Last night!
Olek! Someday I'd like to show him some of the stories
I've written—I'm not a professional like he is, but that
would be the point. To get a professional's opinion.
Burke has read a couple. He got so enthusiastic I didn't
believe him. Then for Christmas, for my stocking—
he gave me *The Writer's Market*, which lists where
I could send—. Of course it didn't fit into my stocking,
but he gave it to me anyway. For some reason that
bothered me. We haven't talked about my stories since.
But Olek... *(Short pause)* Ill bet his wife is lovely.
Beautiful. Black hair. Sultry. And very intellectual.
I think he likes that. In the kitchen he seemed to like
it when I stared at him and nodded, so...I'd love to meet
her. I'd love to go to Poland. And bring things—food,
blankets, sausages. I wouldn't expect a thing from
them. I wouldn't want them to waste their money on
presents, even trinkets. What I'd be doing, I'd be doing

for me. Putting something back into the world, instead
of always taking like we do. Burke would be proud of
me too. *(Beat)* A simple, generous act—made for no
reason but to make it. Made not out of guilt, or to get
something; made without complications. Made pure—
from love. *(Lost in thought:)* My mother used to say to
me, "Mia, whatever I ever say to you, whatever I might
do, whatever you might hear about me, whatever you
find in my closet or bureau when you go snooping,
remember—I love you. If it doesn't sound like love,
or smell like love, or look like love, it doesn't mean
it isn't love, honey, believe me." *(Pause, she is lost
in thought. Suddenly, from the house, the phone rings.
She listens.)* That's the phone. *(She takes off her gardening
gloves, sets them down and hurries off.)*

(End of Scene One)

Scene Two

*(The same. Ten minutes later. MIA enters and begins picking
up her gardening things.)*

MIA: That was—. Olek. From the train station. It seems
the train he was to—. That Burke—. Burke seems
to have just left him there. There's been a mix-up,
obviously. There's a little dot on the timetable—
the train Olek was to take doesn't actually stop here—
today. On Thursdays. So it just—. *(Beat)* Sped by.
And the next train isn't for—. For a long time. He
thought Burke would be...I asked him for coffee.
I didn't want him to have to sit... He's taking a cab.
I said I'd pay. *(Beat)* I called Burke. His line was busy,
so—.

(Phone rings from the house.)

MIA: That must be Burke.

(Pause. MIA *doesn't go. She lets it ring and continues to pick up her things.)*

(End of Scene Two)

Scene Three

(The kitchen. MIA *is making coffee.)*

MIA: *(Pouring water into the pot:)* Burke's not like what some people think he is—he's not a jerk. No way. That's not to say he doesn't have his faults. But give me a break. Any man who misses his daughter as much as he misses his—. *(Beat)* Any father who wants to be with his daughter as much as he wants to be with his daughter—. *(Beat)* I have a lot of time for that. That makes up for a lot of other stuff. No, give me Burke anytime. He's a good guy. Means well. *(Beat)* I don't know how we met; he swears it was when I was waitressing, but I don't remember, really. I was seeing other guys. I was living with a man all the time I was waitressing so... *(Beat)* He was—surprise! A teacher at the New School. We met at the movies. Some things never change, my mother used to say that. He had a terrific apartment in the Village and my daughter had her own room. His wife and two children lived in New Jersey. They knew about us, we knew about them. He taught religion and philosophy so he kept everything above board. *(Beat)* Once they visited, the wife and kids, to go to the Christmas show at Radio City. Everyone stayed in the apartment. Where were we supposed to go, I asked him. Susan and I slept in her room. The kids on the couch. His wife—with him. *(She looks up.)* Somehow this was explained—there wasn't enough mattresses or something; and besides, he said, he should be able to make love to his wife without me getting jealous. *(Beat)* That seemed reasonable. Anyway, Burke came along somewhere

here and... Here I am. I told him that I'd rather be tied
naked on a red ant hill than spend another day of my
life on a college campus, but... Here I am. *(Beat)* The
school system's good. *(Shrug. She finishes making the
coffee, turns it on to start it dripping and waits. She looks
back toward the living room and sighs:)* I don't know how
I got the courage. The man is after all a professional
writer. In Polish, yes, but that still doesn't make him
unprofessional. For me—it's no more than a hobby.
Still, I guess it's a lot better than standing around the
train station rereading the national timetables and
having trains that you think will stop pass by at eighty
miles an hour scaring the hell out of you. *(Smiles)*
Poor man. *(Beat)* I once wrote a story set in the south
of France and I've never even been to Europe. I haven't
even been to Florida. I could have gone to California to
pick grapes but decided I didn't want to do that. *(Beat)*
The story! It's about a child and her mother who's
a painter and she—the mother—falls in love with
the local French doctor. Of course he's French, it's
in France—so all I have to say is: the local doctor.
But the man is already married. *(Beat)* But that's not
the story I gave him to read. I gave him one of my
children's stories that Burke got so excited about.
My daughter loved it too, so—. *(Beat)* Burke said he
saw it with a lot of beautiful illustrations. We looked
at other children's books to see who might be right.
Burke thought the guy who does the scary ones where
everyone looks big and—. There's one about a train
and Santa Claus? Very dark. I don't like dark children's
books. But Burke keeps buying them, even in
hardcover. *(Beat)*

I think the pictures for my story should be colorful
and with a lot of detail. *(She looks toward the living room,
then back at the coffee still dripping out into the pot.)* Some
of it is supposed to be funny. *(She listens, nothing.)* What
possessed me? He walked into the house and nearly the

first thing I say to him—after saying Burke isn't here—
would you read...? *(Beat)* He's been very gracious.
He could have said no. *(Beat)* I wish I could make
cappuccino. When I worked as a waitress I always
enjoyed serving cappuccino; especially to the two tables
that were out on the sidewalk. Very French. Reminded
me of my youth. *(Beat)* My French teacher was the first
to really encourage my writing. I once even wrote a
story in French. That was before I was pregnant. I got
an A-minus. I think that's how he noticed me. Out of
the—. It was a big class. He put a big circle with a smile
on the top of the page. I have it somewhere. In some
trunk in the attic. I remember when I got the story
back—we weren't even asked to write a story—just
some sentences. I did it on my own. It took him two
weeks to grade the papers. On mine, besides the sun
and the grade there was a red ring from a wine glass.
He told me later that he'd kept mine out and read it and
reread it. *(Beat)* Hence—the stain of wine. *(Short pause,
listens, turns back, the coffee is finished.)* I wonder if Olek
reads French. *(Pause, lost in thought, then:)* He didn't
say a word about last night. Not a hint. Maybe he's
embarrassed. Maybe he thinks I would be embarrassed.
I told him last night I wouldn't be. I told him—like
my mother says, some flowers are meant to bloom
only once. *(Beat)* I just didn't want to hurt Burke. *(Beat)*
He agreed with this. *(Short pause)* Then, maybe he was
drunk and doesn't remember. I wondered about that
last night. *(Short pause; sighs)* When Susan was born
and my—the man I had grown up until fifteen thinking
was my father—when he was by my side, telling me to
"breathe-breathe" and "push," the world seemed more
complicated to me than I could bear. *(Beat)* Then Susan
screamed. No, then a baby, my baby screamed, I hadn't
known then what I was going to name her. Nothing
prepared me for what I felt toward that child. You need
such feelings to know why you live. *(Pause)* If you close

yourself off from the primary colors of life. If you're
only seeing things as yellowish and not yellow, blueish
and not blue, then I believe you are not really seeing
life as it is. *(Beat)* That's all I have to say: the extent
of my wisdom of twenty-four long years of life upon
this planet earth. *(Beat)* I wrote her father—the French
teacher—in California and sent him a picture. He said
it took about three months to reach him; he was moving
a lot. But he finally did send her a little Mexican
sombrero that said "Mexico" across the front. I have it
upstairs. The straw kept breaking off so I couldn't let
her play with it, but I did hang it on a wall for a while
so she and I could see it. *(Pause, she pours two cups of
coffee; when she is finished:)* By the way, before-the phone
ringing, that was Susan. She called back. The dean's
daughter asked her to stay for supper. They must be
having a super time together. I said it was okay. *(Beat)*
Burke—he hasn't called. *(She leaves with the coffee.)*

(End of Scene Three)

Scene Four

*(The kitchen. From the living room, the recording of Lena
Horne singing* Stormy Weather *can be heard.* MIA *is
making drinks. She is mouthing along with the song,
swaying, as she opens an ice tray. After some time:)*

MIA: He wanted a drink—with the coffee. I found some
crackers. *(Singing along:)*: "Stormy weather. Since my
love and I ain't together." *(Continuing:)* I'd thought
Reed finished them last night. Burke had put them
away in the wrong cabinet. *(Listens, then looks for
something, finds it and holds it up:)* An ashtray. *(Beat)*
He's been using his coffee saucer. *(Sways to the music:)*
Reed's record. He forgot to take it home. *(Sings with it
for a moment, then:)* Olek loves it. He'd never heard Lena
Horne before last night. *(Stops swaying for a moment, lost*

in thought; music continues.) (Begins to pour the drinks:)
He asked when Burke came home. I said I never knew.
(Beat) But that you can hear his car as soon as it pulls
in—because the driveway's gravel.

(Long pause as the song finishes, when it is over:)

(End of Scene Four)

Scene Five

(The attic; single light bulb. MIA, *towel wound around her
head is looking through a trunk. After a moment, she takes
something out.)*

MIA: Here it is! Look—the wine stain's still there. *(Beat)*
And the circle with the smiling face. *(She opens the folder
and begins to read to herself; looks up:)* Olek said he reads
French, so that's why... *(Goes back and reads to herself,
looks up again:)* There are a lot of words I don't
remember. *(Suddenly remembering:)* Where's the—?
(She thumbs through the folder:) Here it is. He put it
on the last page. *(Holds up the folder for all to see:)* The
A-minus. *(Beat)* I'll take it down to... *(Stops herself, holds
the folder against her chest.)* We used to try to only speak
in French to each other. This was my idea. It made me
feel like I was someone else. Even when we made love
in his apartment, I'd try to speak in French. He was
impressed by that. He said he didn't know I knew so
much. *(Beat)* Why did he—? Me. What did he see in
me? Why—me?? It was a big class, like I said. *(She looks
at her folder:)* I wasn't even one of the better—. Usually,
I was lucky to even get a C. But he picked me. Why?
(Beat) For the first two or three trips to see the foreign
films, we were with a group. A lot of students. Maybe
even another teacher, I don't remember. It was sort of
a club. But then—. Somehow—. It was just us. How
did that happen? Did everyone else just get bored with

foreign films? I wonder. *(Beat)* We spent hours talking,
just him and me. What did he get out of that? I'll bet
I said a lot of stupid things. I always do. And then,
when I said we should speak in—in French. He must
have had the patience of Job. You'd think after a day of
teaching—. He'd want to... *(Shrugs.)* I remember sitting
in his car. He'd stopped to buy cigarettes and I watched
him through the window of the store and he looked
back, saw I was watching him, and he sort of moved his
eyebrows up and down and winked and smiled at me.
He came out with his cigarettes and a single red rose—
how he'd found a rose in what was basically a gas
station I'll never know. *(Beat)* But that was part of
the charm. Where had it come from? He handed me
the rose—maybe we were going to see a movie that
had "rose" in the title but then, I could be putting two
different things together—handed me, of all people, the
rose—and I kissed him. *(Short pause)* And he kissed me.
And I knew that he'd been wanting to do that for ages—
I could tell this. And he put his arm around me and
drew me tight against his chest. Someone honked.
(She laughs.) They wanted to use the gas pump! We
were blocking the gas pumps! *(Laughs)* I held onto his
arm as we drove off to the same movie theater we'd
always gone to, but now it looked completely different.
The movie was in Russian and there wasn't any nudity.
Jim—that's his name, by the way—touched my leg or
thigh at one point, but I stupidly moved away, thinking
I must be crowding him, then realizing too late—. *(Beat)*
We talked about the movie as we always did. He said
he wanted to go to Russia. He said the French language
was very important in Russia and its history. He said
large parts of War and Peace were first written in
French. I did not know that. *(Beat)*

As I've said—a free education. *(Beat)* Later, in his
apartment—I don't know how I got there. Did he ask?
Did I just follow? I'd never been inside his apartment

before. I'd gone by, of course, and seen him washing
his car—all of that, but never before... He had books.
There was a poster from a museum. I don't remember
what it looked like. He said he wouldn't offer me a
glass of wine. He had a futon. *(Beat)* He undressed me.
He unbuttoned my blouse. Pulled down my shorts
and underpants—all very gently. Took off his shirt—
everything, and before kissing me, he put on some
music. *(Suddenly remembering:)* My God, I think it was
Lena Horne! *(Pause. She is lost in thought. Finally:)* What
was it about me that he liked? He was a wonderful
teacher. He taught a lot more than just French. He had
convictions and beliefs. What was there—maybe still
is there—about me? I wish I knew. *(She looks back at the
folder.)* Sometimes, late at night, when neither Susan
nor I can sleep, we'll curl up together in Susan's bed,
stuffed animals and everything, and talk. *(Beat)* Talk. So
often I've wanted at these times to tell her—while we're
hugging—to tell her about what it felt like to me when
I was told that my father wasn't really my father, and
that Herbert and so forth. How, for me, the world
literally spun away. How I was a spaceman suddenly
floating... How—I didn't know where or who I was.
(Beat) All those things I have wanted to say to her.
(Short pause) To help her. To prepare her for the day
when I tell her who her father really is. When she's
older. Perhaps he'll even visit from California. Or
Mexico. *(Beat)* Burke says I'll know when it's the right
time; as a mother I'll feel when it's right. My heart will
tell me, he says. *(She looks back at the folder, then back up
again:)* Olek liked my children's story, by the way.
That's what he said. But he's European, so he's polite.
(Laughs to herself) He said—if he were rich and the
world was a different place, he'd have my story printed
by a printer he knows in Warsaw. This man, he says,
is a great artist. *(Beat)* He also said there was a Polish
illustrator who would be perfect. So he'd like to have

a copy. I'll send him one. He gave me his address. Or
maybe, he said, I could drop one off. *(Beat)* Some day
when I have an excuse to be in the City. *(She adjusts the
towel on her head, then rubs—drying her hair for a moment.
Then explaining:)* We took a shower. *(Pause.)* Olek's
thought many times of writing children's stories
himself—but now, being so far away from his own
children, it would be impossible, he says. *(Beat)* I
wonder why that is. *(Beat)* Anyway, he said he liked
it— "loved it," quote unquote—so... *(She taps the folder:)*
And when I asked—I can't believe I asked, but when
I did—he said: sure, he reads French! "You must be a
glutton for punishment," I said. "That is definitely not
the case," he said. *(Beat)* He told me about the lecture.
What could Burke have been thinking? Olek's
completely embarrassed by the whole thing. He said—
after some prodding on my part, he said—why invite
someone only to humiliate him? *(Beat)* I gather Olek
went to a great deal of trouble getting his translator to
give him a number of different translations for the same
lines in his book. Olek thought the students this way
could see how the same thing could be translated very
differently. He said he wanted the kids to experience
for one morning what he lives with every day of his life.
The "cloud," he said, he lives in. Or the "haze," he said,
you could also call it. But no one seemed the least bit
interested. *(Beat)*

I'm not surprised. Why should we care about a problem
we don't have? That's what most people would think,
anyway. It's probably what I'd think most days. If I
didn't know Olek. *(Beat)* You need to prepare the kids.
And that was Burke's job; so they know what to expect.
Olek says he was amazed when Burke started speaking
without any notes. I told him that's just Burke. With
Burke, you take the good with the bad. I didn't say this,
I didn't think Olek would understand what I meant.
He says the next time Burke asks him up here to talk,

he was going to have to think twice about it before
agreeing. *(Beat)* Fair enough. *(Beat)* His cab should
be here any...I should go back down. *(She doesn't move.*
Short pause) I stopped him when he started making fun
of Burke. Started imitating how he sounds, and that
thing Burke does with his nose and glasses when he
gets excited. I knew he'd gone to a lot of trouble for
Olek. I said, you want to make fun of Burke, go ahead!
A lot of people make fun of him, and he knows that!
It's nothing new! *(Beat)* He shut up after that. At least
about Burke. *(Beat)* Reed, I didn't defend. *(Short pause)*
I suppose it is very hard to be alone in a new country.
You feel—lost. If someone is even just nice to you, you
start thinking they are your good friend. It's confusing.
(Beat) I know what Olek means by living in a "haze"
or "cloud." *(Pause.)* Burke I defended and he shut up.
So many people misunderstand Burke. I think I've
said this before, but it deserves repeating: he's not at
all what he at first seems to be. He's not a jerk. *(Beat)*
His teaching, he takes very, very seriously. Even though
he has tenure. He loves the give and take of it, he says.
I'm sure he's a very generous teacher. He teaches small
classes—which isn't easy, it's where you have to be
yourself. For a long time I remember thinking I could
never love this man—no matter how much I tried to
love him, and I did—I did try. But then one day—it just
happened. I fell in love with Burke. Thank God. It can
be that simple.

(From outside—a car horn.)

MIA: That's the cab. *(She stands up, then turns back:)*
And I think the last thing I would ever want is to see
him hurt. Or even worse—for me to be the one who
hurt him.

(More honking. MIA goes.)

(End of Scene Five)

Scene Six

(The lawn; dusk. Two folding lawn chairs; MIA *sits in one, watching the setting sun.)*

MIA: The world is just as it seems. *(Beat)* It has no other choice. My mother used to say that. And she used to say that talking about your problems won't solve them, in fact, it usually makes them worse. *(Beat)* I tried to argue this point once with her, but as she'd spent most of her life on a college campus and seen firsthand what a lot of talk can do to people, she wouldn't even listen. I told her it's not the same everywhere. She asked me to name one place where it wasn't true. *(Beat)* Talk, talk, talk. Once you've spoken about a problem, she says, it won't be long before you've got it. Words are like germs, and the best way to keep from being infected is to keep your mouth shut. *(Beat)* It's a point of view.

*(*BURKE *enters from the house, holding a book and a drink.)*

BURKE: *(Holding out the book:)* Here.

*(*MIA *reaches for it:)*

BURKE: Don't look at the cover. *(He points to a place on a page:)* Right there.

*(*MIA *looks at the book,* BURKE *smiles.)*

MIA: *(Reads:)* "Over the carnage—?"

*(*BURKE *nods,* MIA *reads:)*

MIA: "Over the carnage rose prophetic a voice.
Be not dishearten'd, affection shall solve the problems of freedom yet,
Those who love each other shall become invincible,
They shall yet make Columbia victorious."

BURKE: *(Taking the book back and putting his hand over the cover:)* That's it.

(Beat)

MIA: So I'm to guess who wrote that?

BURKE: Yeh. *(He smiles.)*

MIA: *(Shrugs:)* I don't know. Someone who goes to Columbia University?

(BURKE bursts out laughing, goes and very patronizingly kisses MIA on the top of her head.)

BURKE: *(As he kisses her:)* Just like my students.

(BURKE sits in the chair, looks out at the sunset, smiling; he sips his drink. MIA looks at him.)

MIA: *(Turns to the audience; BURKE cannot hear this:)* He knows. About Olek. He may not even know he knows, but he does. Of course he's hurt. I knew he would be if he found out. I'm sorry.

(MIA sniffles, BURKE turns to her.)

BURKE: Did you want a drink, I didn't think—.

(MIA shakes her head. BURKE looks at her, then turns away.)

BURKE: *(To the audience; MIA cannot hear this:)* I called my daughter in Sacramento this afternoon. I just felt like it. I forgot all about the time difference, but it turned out that she was home anyway, it'd been a half-day. So we were lucky. *(Beat)* She was happy to hear from me. I couldn't get her off the phone. *(Beat)* She's starting riding lessons. Good for her. She promised she'd be careful. But she's very responsible. *(Beat)* Riding. *(Beat)* So I think she'll really like the Chinese horse I bought at the Metropolitan. *(He turns to MIA:)* If you want to watch T V .

MIA: No. I'm happy out here.

BURKE: *(Smiling:)* Nothing good on?

MIA: I don't know.

BURKE: You don't know what's on T V??!

(BURKE feigns shock, then laughs to himself. MIA looks at him. He sips his drink.)

MIA: How was the lecture?

BURKE: *(Without looking at her:)* Okay. *(Beat)* Banouski got home okay. Back to New York.

(MIA looks at BURKE.)

BURKE: I just called him. Olek Banouski. Who was here last night? I called to see if he got home okay. *(Beat)* You bring a man up here—. You feel responsible. *(Beat)*

MIA: And he got home okay?

BURKE: Yes. *(Pause.)*

MIA: *(To audience:)* Susan should be home any minute.

BURKE: *(To audience:)* I spent the afternoon with Reed. Holding Reed's hand. *(He smiles.)* He needed someone to talk to—and I was there. *(Beat)* I'm his friend. He and Barbara are getting married. They decided over lunch today. So it wasn't that he was holding her off—. That was more of a mutual thing. He thought she could just move up here—like Mia moved up here—in fact he said he used us as an example to Barbara. But Barbara said only if they got married. She doesn't trust him, I think. Good for her.

(BURKE to himself. MIA looks at him.)

MIA: What's funny?

(BURKE turns and looks at MIA, then "hears" her question and answers:)

BURKE: "Someone who goes to Columbia University." *(He smiles and sips his drink.)*

MIA: *(To the audience:)* So who the hell wrote it, as if I care?

BURKE: *(To audience, continuing:)* So he said it all came to a head last night while they were driving here. So that's why—if he seemed a little preoccupied, he said... *(Beat)* He said he hoped he hadn't been rude or anything to Olek; if he had it was because he was tense because of... He says he doesn't remember anything he said. *(Beat)* And I thought he'd just gotten fed up with Banouski. *(Beat)* That's probably why Barbara didn't complain about the smoke—she probably didn't even notice, because she was somewhere else. *(Beat)* Married. They want children, he says. And the school system up here is pretty good. My daughter got a damn good education here. While she was here. I had no complaints, and being a teacher I should—. *(Beat)* My daughter can't come this summer, she said, because of the riding lessons. I told her there are plenty of horses here! *(Beat)* I think there must also be a boy.

MIA: Mind if I have a sip?

(It takes a moment for BURKE to hear this, then he hands MIA his drink. She sips. He looks at her, then turns to the audience.)

BURKE: *(To the audience:)* Why did I make fun of her? I know she doesn't like it. I should know better.

MIA: *(To audience, as she sips:)* He hates me. I hurt him and he hates me. Fair enough. *(Beat)* Please God, don't let him throw me out.

BURKE: *(To the audience:)* Dear God—don't let her leave me!

(Car honks.)

MIA: Finally! It's Susan. I was getting worried. *(She stands and waves.)*

BURKE: *(Standing:)* So was I.

(BURKE *and* MIA *wave to Susan.)*

END OF PLAY

www.ingramcontent.com/pod-product-compliance
Lightning Source LLC
Chambersburg PA
CBHW070032110426
42741CB00035B/2745